Focus on the Prayer Book
An Adult Study Program for Forming Faith

Phrases in Threes

- *Discovering meaning*
- *Discerning direction*
- *Deepening faith*
  Through exploration
  of the liturgy

Nancy Dering Martin

MOREHOUSE PUBLISHING
A Continuum imprint
HARRISBURG • LONDON • NEW YORK

Morehouse Publishing
P.O. Box 1321
Harrisburg, Pennsylvania 17105

Morehouse Publishing is a Continuum imprint.

Cover design by Trude Brummer

Library of Congress Cataloging-in-Publication Data

Martin, Nancy Dering.
    Phrases in threes : discovering meaning, discerning direction, and
deepening faith through exploration of the Liturgy / Nancy Dering
Martin.
        p.   cm. -- (Focus on the prayer book)
    ISBN 0-8192-1943-6
    1. Episcopal Church Book of common prayer. 2. Christian
life--Anglican authors. I. Title.
    BX5945 .M37 2003
    264'.03'00715--dc21
                                                2002153545

03   04   05   06   07   08   6   5   4   3   2   1

CONTENTS

INTRODUCTION

"In the beginning was the Word, and the Word was with God, and the Word was God."

—John 1:1

Words. I love them. In particular, I am intrigued by how deceptively small words can convey such large ideas: Peace, Sin, Unity. And how large words can convey such enormous ideas: Redemption. Salvation. Reconciliation.

Except for the Holy Scriptures, there is perhaps no more profound nor lyric source of small words with huge meanings than the Book of Common Prayer. Crafted exquisitely, with elegance and economy, the liturgy is a wonderful compendium of the prayers, confessions, and blessings that are the rubric of our personal and corporate worship.

But, as with many words recited frequently, the meaning of these words is often in peril of becoming so rote as to be spoken without thinking, repeated without reflection.

The Greek roots of *liturgy* are *leos* (people) + *ergon* (work), which means that liturgy is the work of the people. But the people have other work to do, too —and exploring the meaning of the words of the liturgy is a useful spiritual task. This book and the series of which it is a part are designed to do just that.

This book of meditations is based on six passages taken from various segments of The Book of Common Prayer. Their use is by no means limited, however, to Episcopalians; the concepts and the prayers they are based on are timeless and universal for all Christians. Each passage consists of three phrases, which will be considered separately and in combination. The six chapters or lessons are designed to be examined and explored in one-hour group discussions, but may also be used as individual meditations or devotions.

Each lesson is self-contained, not based on those that precede or follow it, allowing for flexibility in scheduling. Each session is developed with relevant scripture passages and discussion questions and is designed to be led by a facilitator. The facilitator's role, with some preparation, is not to teach, but rather to assist the group in examining and exploring the words and to encourage the participants to support and challenge one another in the exploration. Groups may choose to rotate the assignment of a facilitator among various members.

GETTING THE MOST FROM GROUP DISCUSSIONS

As you make your way through these lessons, you'll be encouraged to discover meaning, discern direction, and, ultimately, deepen your faith. This process of self-guided learning and discernment can be a powerful force in both individual and group spiritual growth. Its power can be enhanced (or diminished, unfortunately) by the dynamics in the group. ***Here are a few ways to contribute to a powerful learning environment and get the most from this series:***

1. Participate fully.

Your group's depth of exploration is proportionate to the richness of participation. If, for example, a few people do all the talking, the group is disadvantaged by not hearing a broad array of ideas. Speak up and make a conscious attempt to share your thoughts. Share examples from your own experience. If some group members are silent, ignored, or excluded, make a sincere attempt to invite their participation, respecting the fact that some people would prefer simply to listen.

2. Listen thoughtfully and look for opportunities to learn from one another.

This is a challenge, especially if others see things differently. Allow others to finish their thoughts before responding. Ask for clarification and elaboration when others share ideas you don't understand. And learn to regard every statement you don't agree with as a learning opportunity, responding with more curiosity than certainty. Ask others to help you understand, and be open to new and different perspectives. This is what exploration is all about.

3. Accept shared responsibility for your group's success.

Sometimes participants expect the group's facilitator to take care of everything. But that won't work here. Come prepared to focus and participate. Help others in the group if they are lost or confused. Volunteer to look up and read the Scripture passages. Try to review the material and reflect before your group meets. Accept and prepare for the role of facilitator when your turn rolls around.

4. Take time to collect your thoughts and reflect.

After your group meets, summarize your new insights. Jot down ideas that you'd like to think about or discuss further. You may want to include new insights in a journal or prayer for more illumination and understanding. Try some of the extension activities suggested after each lesson.

LESSON 1

"... source of all good desires, all right judgments, and all just works ..."

OPENING PRAYER

Most holy God, the source of all good desires, all right judgments, and all just works: Give to us, your servants, that peace which the world cannot give, so that our minds may be fixed on the doing of your will, and that we, delivered from the fear of all enemies, may live in peace and quietness; through the mercies of Christ Jesus our Savior. Amen.

INTRODUCTION

This set of three phrases appears in the Collect for Peace on page 123 of the Book of Common Prayer. In it, we ask, "Most holy God, *the source of all good desires, all right judgments, and all just works,* Give to us, your servants, that peace which the world cannot give, so that our minds may be fixed on the doing of your will ..."

Read the Collect aloud, listening carefully for the theme of peace. Think about what peace means to you. How do you find it? How do you keep it? Today, we'll let the words of the Book of Common Prayer lead us to a deeper understanding of peace, as we explore God as the source of all good desires, right judgments, and just works that lead us to peace.

ALL GOOD DESIRES

Begin by reflecting on our many different kinds of desires.

What are some of our desires? What are their sources?

_____

_____

_____

_____

_____

_____

_____

_____

_____

_____

_____

Webster defines *desire* as a "wish" or "craving". We know from experience that our desires can be for any things from world peace to petty revenge, from sex to shoes. In this passage, we're acknowledging God as the source of *"all **good** desires."*

The Bible includes the word *desire* over 100 times, split almost evenly between the Old and New Testaments. Read the following Scripture verses and jot down your reactions:

GENESIS 3:16

_____

_____

_____

_____

PSALM 112:10

_____

_____

_____

_____

LUKE 5:39

_____

_____

_____

_____

1. What are the various meanings and types of *desires* referenced in these readings? How do they compare with the types and sources of desires you reflected on?

_____

_____

_____

_____

_____

2. In light of the Scripture you've just read, what could *all good desires* include?

_____

_____

_____

_____

_____

3. In a prayer asking for peace, what *good desires* would you include? How would these good desires help bring about peace?

_____

_____

_____

_____

_____

_____

ALL RIGHT JUDGMENTS

Next, we acknowledge God as the source of *all right judgments. Judgments* are decisions, authoritative conclusions, and opinions. Chances are, you're on the giving or receiving end of dozens of judgments every day.

In this prayer, though, we're acknowledging *God*—not human beings—as the source of all the right judgments that we make.

4. Reflect on examples of good and bad judgments. Take a look at some of the judgments you've made and received. Consider ones you've read about, in books and in the news, as well as the ones you've observed through the experiences of your family and friends. What does *judgment* mean to you personally?

_____

_____

_____

_____

_____

In the Bible, the word *judgment* appears over 100 times, mostly in the Old Testament. Let's turn to Scripture now. Read the following, listening carefully and jotting down your thoughts:

GENESIS 39:10-20

_____

_____

_____

_____

ESTHER 5:11-14

_____

_____

_____

_____

Luke 7:38-50

_____

_____

_____

_____

5. How do these Scripture passages expand your understanding of human judgment?

_____

_____

_____

_____

6. Keeping these Scriptures in mind, what are some examples of *all right judgments?* In a prayer for peace, what "right judgments" would you include? How would these judgments contribute to, or help bring about, peace?

_____

_____

_____

_____

ALL JUST WORKS

Webster defines *works* as "acts or deeds," usually used in the plural, as in *good works.* Another way of saying *just* is "proper" or "right."

7. What does *just works* mean to you? Again, consider examples from your own life, from works of literature or film, or even from the news.

_____

_____

_____

_____

_____

8. Let's see what Scripture has to say about *just works*. Read these passages and jot down your response:

MATTHEW 5:16

_____

_____

_____

_____

MATTHEW 7:22

_____

_____

_____

_____

MATTHEW 16:27

_____

_____

_____

_____

_____

_____

_____

_____

_____

9. With these works of Scripture in mind, reflect on examples of *just works*. In a prayer for peace, what examples of just works would you include? How would these works help bring about peace?

_____

_____

_____

_____

_____

_____

_____

_____

_____

PUTTING IT ALL TOGETHER

When we consider the phrases together, we are acknowledging God as the *source of all good desires, all right judgments, and all just works*, in preparation for asking for peace, that our minds may be "fixed on the doing of your will." This is an acknowledgment of grand proportion, suggesting our understanding of the awesome power of God and our total reliance on God as the source of all that is good, right, and just. We seek his providence in supplying us—individually and collectively—with the *good desires, right judgments, and just works* that will ultimately bring about peace.

10. What, for you, has become more clear as a result of exploring this segment of the Collect for Peace? For example, what have you discovered about the sources and conditions of peace? How can an attitude of peace make us more open to discerning—and following—God's will?

_____

_____

_____

_____

11. Reflect on this discussion and your own insights, and write your own prayer for peace. Include specific ways in your own life that you can acknowledge God as the source of desires, judgments, and good works.

_____

_____

_____

_____

IN THE DAYS AND WEEKS AHEAD . . .

Reflect on this Collect for Peace and consider the following:

- Be alert for good desires, right judgments, and just works and jot down examples.

- Look for current events or news articles that illustrate good desires, right judgments, and just works. Clip them out and share them with the group at our next meeting.

- Increase others' awareness of the relationship between good desires, right judgments, and just works with peace through conversation. As you interact with others every day, don't be afraid to point out ways that good desires, right judgments, and just works help bring about peace at home, in the workplace, and in the world.

LESSON 2

". . . constantly speak the truth, boldly rebuke vice, and patiently suffer for truth's sake . . ."

OPENING PRAYER

Almighty God, by whose providence thy servant John the Baptist was wonderfully born, and sent to prepare the way of thy Son our Savior by preaching repentance: Make us so to follow his doctrine and holy life, that we may truly repent according to his preaching; and after his example constantly speak the truth, boldly rebuke vice, and patiently suffer for the truth's sake; through the same thy Son Jesus Christ our Lord, who liveth and reigneth with thee and the Holy Spirit, one God for ever and ever. Amen.

INTRODUCTION

Among the traditional collects for Holy Days, we find the collect appointed for the Nativity of Saint John the Baptist on June 24 (page 190). John the Baptist, a cousin of Jesus, was the "voice that cried out in the wilderness," fearlessly preaching repentance and preparing the way for the Messiah.

This prayer asks God to *make* us model our lives after John the Baptist and to follow his example in three ways: by speaking the truth, by rebuking vice, and by suffering for truth's sake. Each of these ways is further emphasized and enlivened with a strong adverb: *constantly* speak the truth, *boldly* rebuke vice, and *patiently* suffer for truth's sake.

Let's explore each "way" individually, linking it to the example of John the Baptist—and to ourselves.

CONSTANTLY SPEAK THE TRUTH

Have you ever felt compelled to speak an unwelcome truth? What does constantly speaking the truth mean to you? What are some of the consequences?

_____

_____

_____

_____

Beyond veracity, the "truth" in the New Testament is used to describe the character and revelation of God. With this meaning in mind, turn to the New Testament and read John 5:31-33.

What was the "truth" that John the Baptist was preaching? What does this verse tell you about what it means to "speak the truth?"

_____

_____

_____

_____

1. How does this verse illuminate the request to make us *constantly speak the truth?* Think about ways that speaking the truth in your life can help you imitate the "holy life" of John the Baptist.

_____

_____

_____

_____

BOLDLY REBUKE VICE

Next, the collect asks that God *make* us follow John's example of *boldly rebuking vice.* Read another passage from Matthew 14:3-4.

2. What does this passage tell you about the imperative and perils of *boldly rebuking vice?*

_____

_____

_____

_____

3. What are the contemporary parallels to John's example? As you think about your home, your church, your workplace—or even our society—consider situations where we should be boldly rebuking vice. What are the costs and rewards of doing so?

_____

_____

_____

_____

_____

PATIENTLY SUFFER FOR TRUTH'S SAKE

4. John the Baptist's ministry is fearless and resourceful. And even though he's thrown in prison—and eventually beheaded—he remains faithful to God until the very end.

   Read Matthew 14:5-12

   What good does John's patient suffering accomplish? What can we learn from it?

_____

_____

_____

_____

_____

5. Are there modern-day John the Baptists? What contemporary figures constantly speak the truth, boldly rebuke vice, and suffer patiently for the truth? How do their examples speak to us as Christians of today?

_____

_____

_____

_____

_____

_____

PUTTING IT ALL TOGETHER

". . . constantly speak the truth, boldly rebuke vice, and patiently suffer for truth's sake . . ."

6. When taken together, what are we asking when we ask God to *make us so follow his (John's) doctrine and holy life . . . ?"* What would our speaking and rebuking and suffering look like if our prayer were answered?

_____

_____

_____

_____

_____

_____

7. How can we translate this into our daily realities and responsibilities in the weeks and months ahead?

_____

_____

_____

_____

_____

CLOSING PRAYER

Father, in the words of John the Baptist, "A man can receive only what is given him from heaven." We request your strength, your guidance, and your grace in following his example to constantly speak the truth, boldly rebuke vice, and patiently suffer for truth's sake. Reveal to us those situations where we are called to follow his holy life. Amen.

IN THE DAYS AND WEEKS AHEAD . . .

Reflect on this Collect for the Nativity of Saint John the Baptist and consider the following:

- Reflect on biblical and historical figures who have exhibited these characteristics. Consider the conviction, the courage, and the sacrifice that marked the lives of Saint John the Baptist, the saints, the martyrs, and others.

- Keep a journal of insights and observations about contemporary people who speak the truth or rebuke vice or suffer for truth's sake. Observe the commitment of these people. Why do they do what they do? How do these behaviors change their lives or those of people around them?

- Look for current events or news articles that illustrate speaking the truth, rebuking vice, or suffering for truth's sake. Clip them out and share them with the group at our next meeting.

- Look for opportunities to exhibit these behaviors. Consider why you or others decide to speak up, rebuke vice, or suffer for truth's sake, and why you or others decide not to. Is there a price for not seizing these opportunities? Who pays it?

LESSON 3

"...strengthen the faithful, arouse the careless, and restore the penitent..."

OPENING PRAYER

Almighty and everliving God, ruler of all things in heaven and earth, hear our prayers for this parish family. Strengthen the faithful, arouse the careless, and restore the penitent. Grant us all things necessary for our common life, and bring us all to be of one heart and mind within your holy Church; through Jesus Christ our Lord. Amen.

INTRODUCTION

Among the prayers for the Church is a wonderful prayer for the parish (page 817) that asks God to "grant all things necessary for our common life and bring us all to be of one heart and mind within your Holy Church." Within this prayer, we ask God to *strengthen the faithful, arouse the careless, and restore the penitent.* In just ten words, this prayer captures a large part of the mission of a parish. If, indeed, this is the work of parish strengthening, what are we asking for?

STRENGTHEN THE FAITHFUL

The strengthening of already faithful people is an interesting request.

1. As a person of faith, have you ever felt the need for further strengthening? What were the circumstances?

_____

_____

_____

_____

_____

_____

2. What role do we play—on our own and as a parish family—in *strengthening the faithful?* What responsibilities do we have individually and collectively?

_____

_____

_____

_____

AROUSE THE CARELESS

This is a curious request. In the Bible, there are several references to *carelessness*. Jot down your reactions to these passages from the Old Testament:

ISAIAH 47:1-11

_____

_____

_____

_____

EZEKIEL 30:9

_____

_____

_____

_____

EZEKIEL 39:6

_____

_____

_____

_____

_____

_____

_____

_____

3. How do these passages clarify who among our parish family, including ourselves, comprise the *careless*?

_____

_____

_____

_____

_____

4. What can we do—as individuals and as a parish family—to *arouse the careless?*

_____

_____

_____

_____

_____

RESTORE THE PENITENT

The Scriptures make several references to the restoration of the penitent. Jot down your reflections on the following passage:

_____

_____

_____

_____

5. What does Job learn about penitence? What promises of restoration and reward does God make to him? What does this passage show us about how to treat others who repent of their sins?

_____

_____

_____

_____

_____

6. Consider the concept of restoration. To what are the penitent restored? How will restoring the penitent bring "us all to be of one heart and mind within your holy Church?" Have you ever been welcomed back—or "restored"—after an absence or a transgression? Have you ever welcomed back someone else? Think about ways this event affected your relationship.

_____

_____

_____

_____

_____

_____

PUTTING IT ALL TOGETHER

". . . strengthen the faithful, arouse the careless, and restore the pentitent . . ."

When taken together, these three requests combine to make a powerful statement of the call to corporate worship, service, and mutual life in Christ.

7. How do I answer this call? How does our parish answer this call?

_____

_____

_____

_____

_____

_____

_____

8. What should I—and my parish—do differently?

_____

_____

_____

_____

_____

_____

_____

CLOSING PRAYER

Oh God, who gives us what we need, help our parish to discern your way and will for us and to seek opportunities to *strengthen the faithful, arouse the careless, and restore the penitent.* Give us guidance individually and collectively to continually strengthen our parish family. Amen.

IN THE DAYS AND WEEKS AHEAD . . .

Reflect on this Prayer for the Parish and consider the following:

- Be alert for opportunities to strengthen the faithful, arouse the careless, and restore the penitent.

- Consider these admonitions during the routines of the parish life, particularly meetings.

- Look for churches whose parish life and programs exemplify strengthening the faithful, arousing the careless, or restoring the penitent. Begin a dialogue with others in your church about ways of integrating these ideas into the fabric of your own parish.

- Look for small, easy ways to strengthen the faithful, such as sending a quick note or email of appreciation to someone in your parish who is working tirelessly in the nursery, or tending the flowerbeds, or putting out the newsletter.

LESSON 4

". . . bless our land with honorable industry, sound learning, and pure manners . . ."

OPENING PRAYER

Almighty God, who hast given us this good land for our heritage: We humbly beseech thee that we may always prove ourselves a people mindful of thy favor and glad to do thy will. Bless our land with honorable industry, sound learning, and pure manners. Save us from violence, discord, and confusion; from pride and arrogance, and from every evil way. Defend our liberties, and fashion into one united people the multitudes brought hither out of many kindreds and tongues. Endue with the spirit of wisdom those to whom in thy Name we entrust the authority of government, that there may be justice and peace at home, and that, through obedience to thy law, we may show forth thy praise among the nations of the earth. In the time of prosperity, fill our hearts with thankfulness, and in the day of trouble, suffer not our trust in thee to fail; all which we ask through Jesus Christ our Lord. Amen.

INTRODUCTION

Within the Prayers and Thanksgiving are the Prayers for National Life, and a prayer for "our Country" (page 820). Within it, we ask God to *bless our land with honorable industry, sound learning, and pure manners.* For what, exactly, are we asking? Why would we seek these blessings for our country?

HONORABLE INDUSTRY

Beyond the usual meaning that we associate with the word *industry*—commerce, business, gross domestic product, and the engine that fuels a nation's economy—*industry* can also refer to diligence and the dignity associated with work done willingly and done well. That's how the word is used here.

Turn to these Scriptural passages and reflect on how they relate to *industry:*

PROVERBS 31:12-25

_____

_____

_____

PROVERBS 10:5

_____

_____

_____

_____

1 TIMOTHY 5:8

_____

_____

_____

_____

I KINGS 11:28

_____

_____

_____

_____

1. How do these passages help define and clarify *honorable industry?* Why is this so important for individuals? Why is it desirable for our country?

_____

_____

_____

_____

2. Beyond asking God to "Bless our land with *honorable industry*," what is the role of the Church in assuring honorable industry? Does the church have a prophetic role to play in speaking out for the just treatment of workers? What responsibilities do individuals have in this regard?

_____

_____

_____

_____

_____

_____

SOUND LEARNING

Learning is defined as "acquiring knowledge through experience or instruction." The words *learn, learned,* and *learning* appear dozens of times in the Bible.

Consider the following Scripture verses with references to learning. Jot down your reactions:

PROVERBS 9:9

_____

_____

_____

MICAH 4:1-4

_____

_____

_____

_____

_____

_____

_____

_____

3. What do these passages illustrate about the kinds of learning that are sound? How does sound learning bless a nation? How does our nation honor the commitment to sound learning?

_____

_____

_____

_____

_____

_____

4. What role has the Church historically played is assuring *sound learning* in our nation? What role should it play today?

_____

_____

_____

_____

_____

_____

PURE MANNERS

In this context, the word *manners* refers less to "etiquette" and more to the behaviors, conduct, and customs of a nation's culture.

Turn to the following Bible verses and jot down the ways they inform about pure manners.

LEVITICUS 20:23

_____

_____

_____

_____

ACTS 25:16

_____

_____

_____

_____

5. Using this definition and the Scriptural references, what are the *manners* of our country? Why are pure manners important to a nation?

_____

_____

_____

_____

_____

6. If our requests to be blessed with *pure manners* were granted, what would the conduct and customs of our culture look like? What differences would we see?

_____

_____

_____

_____

_____

7. What is the role of the Church in assuring *pure manners* in our nation?

_____

_____

_____

_____

_____

PUTTING IT ALL TOGETHER

". . . bless our land with honorable industry, sound learning, and pure manners . . ."

We ask these blessings of God—honorable industry, sound learning, and pure manners—as we seek to become a people aware of God's bounty and eager to do his will.

8. In America, which respects religious diversity and carefully separates church and state, how can we seek out God's will for our nation? How can we reconcile our understanding of God's will with that of other groups who may see things differently?

CLOSING PRAYER

Lord, you challenge us to use the wisdom, authority, unity, liberty, and justice that are available to us to "show forth thy praise among the nations of the earth." Help us to wisely use your many blessings to you, glory. Amen.

IN THE DAYS AND WEEKS AHEAD . . .

Reflect on this Collect for our Country and consider the following:

- Paraphrase this collect. Try to put it in your own words.

   Read or sing the words to Hymn 718. Reflect on what the lyricist, Daniel Crane Roberts, is asking for our country. Are there similarities to the collect?

- Look for current events or news articles that illustrate organizations, churches, or individuals who have a commitment to honorable industry, sound learning, or pure manners. Take note of what underlies their commitment. Clip articles and share them with the group at our next meeting.

- Send an email or letter to your local, state, or federal representatives, expressing your specific views on how our society can benefit from honorable industry, sound learning, and pure manners.

LESSON 5

". . . barriers which divide us may crumble, suspicions disappear, hatreds cease . . ."

OPENING PRAYER

Grant, O God, that your holy and life-giving Spirit may so move every human heart (and especially the hearts of the people of this land), that barriers which divide us may crumble, suspicions disappear, and hatreds cease; that our divisions being healed, we may live in justice and peace; through Jesus Christ our Lord. Amen.

INTRODUCTION

This Prayer for Social Justice (page 823) is awesome in both its scope and its economy—in just ten words, it expresses what we are asking the "life-giving Spirit to move every human heart" to do.

. . . THAT BARRIERS WHICH DIVIDE US MAY CRUMBLE

This first request suggests that after moving "every human heart" (and especially the hearts of the people of this land), the *barriers which divide us* will crumble.

John refers to "division" several times. Read the following verses from John and jot down your responses.

JOHN 7:43

_____

_____

_____

_____

_____

_____

JOHN 9:16

_____

_____

_____

_____

JOHN 10:19

_____

_____

_____

_____

1. What are the types of divisions John is describing?

_____

_____

_____

_____

_____

2. What are the *barriers that divide us* as a society?

_____

_____

_____

_____

3. What would it take for these barriers to crumble?

_____

_____

_____

_____

_____

4. What is the role of the Church in this crumbling of barriers? What is the responsibility of Christians in *crumbling the barriers?*

_____

_____

_____

_____

_____

SUSPICIONS DISAPPEAR

5. What are the *suspicions* that threaten unity and impede justice and peace—within our personal relationships, our country, and our world? What are the underlying causes of those suspicions?

_____

_____

_____

_____

_____

6. What would it take to make these suspicions *disappear?* What role does the Church play in making this happen?

_____

_____

_____

_____

_____

_____

HATREDS CEASE

There are several references to *hatred* in both the Old and the New Testaments. Read the following and note your responses:

EZEKIEL 35:5-11

_____

_____

_____

_____

GALATIANS 5:19-21

_____

_____

_____

_____

7. What are the hatreds referred to in these verses? How does hatred threaten our personal relationships? Our neighborhoods and workplaces? Our nation and the world?

_____

_____

_____

_____

_____

_____

8. What can you do to make the hatreds *cease?* What can the Christian community do?

_____

_____

_____

_____

_____

_____

9. What is the role of the Church in making these hatreds cease in our community? Our nation? Our world?

_____

_____

_____

_____

_____

_____

_____

_____

PUTTING IT ALL TOGETHER

". . . barriers which divide may crumble, suspicions disappear, hatred cease . . ."

In the closing of this prayer, we get a glimpse of the outcome of the Spirit moving every human heart: "That our divisions being healed, we may live in justice and peace."

10. Beyond *praying*, what are we called to do to make this vision a reality?

_____

_____

_____

_____

_____

_____

_____

CLOSING PRAYER

Help us to envision a nation and a world where divisions are healed and where we will live in justice and peace. And help us to discern our role in making barriers to this vision a reality: making barriers crumble, making suspicions disappear, and making hatreds cease. Amen.

IN THE DAYS AND WEEKS AHEAD . . .

Reflect on this Collect for Social Justice and consider the following:

- Be alert for examples of the life-giving Spirit moving a human heart (yours and another's).

- Look for news articles that illustrate work that breaks down barriers to social justice, acts that make suspicions disappear, or words or actions aimed at making hatreds cease. Consider who is doing this work. Clip the articles out and share them with the group at our next meeting.

- Find out what your parish is doing to eliminate injustice in your community and consider contributing or volunteering.

- In your prayers, ask for wisdom and courage to break down barriers, eradicate suspicions, and make hatreds cease.

- Look for movies that address themes of social justice. Invite friends to watch them with you and use them as a springboard to discussion.

LESSON 6

". . . so guide our minds, so fill our imaginations, and so control our wills . . ."

OPENING PRAYER

Almighty and eternal God, so draw our hearts to thee, so guide our minds, so fill our imaginations, so control our wills, that we may be wholly thine, utterly dedicated unto thee; and then use us, we pray thee, as thou wilt, and always to thy glory and the welfare of thy people; through our Lord and Savior Jesus Christ. Amen.

INTRODUCTION

Within the Prayers and Thanksgivings, specifically those for Personal and Family Life, is this prayer for self-dedication (pages 832-833). The prayer asks God to "draw our hearts to thee, *so guide our minds, so fill our imaginations, so control our wills,* as we seek God's glory and the welfare of God's people.

Self-dedication is an intriguing concept, connoting personal recommitment to praise and service. These three requests, then, are a precursor to being wholly God's and utterly dedicated to God.

SO GUIDE OUR MINDS

The definition of *mind* is "the reasoning facility of an individual." It can also pertain to memory and intention. Read the following Scripture passages and jot down the ways that each relates to our capacity to reason:

    LUKE 9:47

_____

_____

_____

_____

TITUS 3:1-3

_____

_____

_____

ROMANS 7:23-25

_____

_____

_____

1. What do these passages tell us about the use of our intellects—our minds—in
    our relationship with God? Do you see your relationship with God as intellectual
    or emotional—or a combination of both?

_____

_____

_____

_____

SO FILL OUR IMAGINATIONS

What a delightful and, to some, unexpected request! To some people, imagination can be
a dangerous thing—perhaps something to be avoided, to prevent frivolous thoughts, or,
worse yet, mischief. In the Bible, _imagination_ refers both to the wonderful mental capacity to envision and to the potential to create mayhem.

Compare and contrast the following passages:

List A	List B
Genesis 6:5	Jeremiah 3:17
Romans 1:21	Proverbs 6:18

_____

_____

_____

_____

_____

2. What do you think *imagination* means in the context of this prayer? How does your imagination nurture your relationship with God? How does it hinder that relationship?

_____

_____

_____

_____

_____

SO CONTROL OUR WILLS

The word *will,* as a noun meaning "*intention*" or "*wish*", is mentioned in the Bible dozens of times, with most of the references in the New Testament.

Reflect on the following Scripture passage and jot down how it illuminates your understanding of the notion of will:

_____

_____

_____

_____

3. What does this passage tell you about the role that our wills play in self-dedication? What does it suggest about controlling our unruly wills?

_____

_____

_____

_____

_____

_____

PUTTING IT ALL TOGETHER

". . . so guide our minds, so fill our imaginations, and so control our wills . . ."

Reflect on the three requests together.

4. Use your imagination: How would your thoughts, actions, decisions, or behavior differ, if indeed God granted you these requests? How would you be a different person? In what way would your life change?

_____

_____

_____

_____

_____

CLOSING PRAYER

Dear Lord, we contemplate rededication of our lives to be utterly, totally yours. So guide us, fill us, and control us that we may experience the rekindling of your spirit within us. Amen.

IN THE DAYS AND WEEKS AHEAD . . .

Reflect on this Prayer for Self-Dedication and consider the following:

- Reflect on the gifts of mind, imagination, and will. Explore ways in which your mind, your imagination, and your will are assets for serving God and others.

- Identify individuals who have dedicated themselves to God and engage them in a conversation on how they continually re-dedicate themselves.

- Read or sing the words to Hymn 694. How are the gifts of mind, imagination, and will expressed in these words?

- Reflect on just how open you are to having your imagination filled. Can you imagine what it was like to live in the time of Christ? Can you envision the kingdom of God? Can you allow your imagination to be filled with the possibilities of God's love?

USING *PHRASES IN THREES*: HINTS FOR FACILITATORS

Objective: Throughout the Book of Common Prayer, there are sentences that include phrases in threes. This book will enable participants to examines six of these passages and deepen their understanding of these often-recited but seldom-explored phrases.

Theme: You may want to reiterate this theme of threes at the beginning of each lesson and ask the participants to identify other things that occur in threes. Communication experts agree that three is the number of items most readily recalled; this may make your group's discussions memorable.

These lessons require one hour to complete.

LESSON 1: ". . . SOURCE OF GOOD DESIRES, ALL RIGHT JUDGMENTS, AND ALL JUST WORKS . . ."

This lesson is based on the Collect for Peace, so you can't go wrong by continually bringing the group back to the concept of peace. You may want to have your group identify examples of discord in home, work, or church. Or, you might clip examples of current domestic or international strife from the newspaper and relate these examples to the theme of this lesson.

This prayer also emphasizes God as the source of the conditions for or precursors to peace: good desires, right judgments, and just works. This can open an interesting conversation regarding the people of God as *instruments* of peace, referring to the well-known words of St. Francis of Assisi, "Lord, make me an instrument of your peace." Your group might discuss what kinds of desires, judgments, and just works are necessary to restore harmony in the examples they cited for home, work, or church. Or, you may want to direct the same discussion to the domestic or international examples and what it would take to bring about peace.

LESSON 2: ". . . CONSTANTLY SPEAK THE TRUTH, BOLDLY REBUKE VICE, AND PATIENTLY SUFFER FOR THE TRUTH'S SAKE . . ."

This lesson is taken from the prayer for the Nativity of Saint John the Baptist. In preparation for the session, you may want to brush up on the life and martyrdom of John the Baptist. You can't go wrong by bringing the discussion back to the example of John the Baptist and what we can learn from his life about speaking the truth, rebuking vice, and patiently suffering for truth's sake.

You may want to engage the group in discussions of other Christian martyrs, including St. Stephen, St. Joan of Arc, or others. Or, you may want to discuss contemporary figures whose lives and writings have exemplified speaking the truth and patiently suffering for truth's sake. Examples may include Dietrich Bonhoffer, Martin Luther King, Jr., Nelson Mandela, Mahatma Gandhi, Jimmy Carter, and others.

LESSON 3: ". . . STRENGTHEN THE FAITHFUL, AROUSE THE CARELESS, AND RESTORE THE PENITENT . . ."

This phrase comes from a prayer for the parish and can be a wonderful discussion starter for exploring the mission of the Church in general and a parish in particular. You might want to engage the group in a discussion of the programs and services of your parish that exemplify each of the three phrases. For example, sessions such as this one are an excellent way to *strengthen the faithful*. Use caution to keep this discussion positive and forward-looking. It may be tempting for a group to lament the high cost of building maintenance rather than explore more important issues.

LESSON 4: ". . . BLESS OUR LAND WITH HONORABLE INDUSTRY, SOUND LEARNING, AND PURE MANNERS . . ."

This lesson is based on a prayer of thanksgiving for National Life, a theme rich in current examples. In preparation for this session, you may want to look for examples of honorable industry, sound learning, and pure manners—or the lack thereof. Again, use care to keep the conversation focused on the blessings that we are requesting and what role the church should and could play in pursuing and assuring each.

LESSON 5: ". . . BARRIERS WHICH DIVIDE MAY CRUMBLE, SUSPICIONS DISAPPEAR, HATREDS CEASE . . ."

This lesson is also rich in current domestic and international examples. Before the session, you might clip newspaper articles that illustrate barriers, suspicions, or hatred on many levels. Or, you might give your group this assignment the week prior to this session and ask the group to brainstorm definitions for "social order" and "social justice."

Then, relate the phrases to their definitions. An important theme in this lesson is the "moving of every human heart." Try to bring the conversations back to that idea and relate the idea of individual transformation to the concepts of social order and social justice.

LESSON 6: ". . . SO GUIDE OUR MINDS, SO FILL OUR IMAGINATIONS AND SO CONTROL OUR WILLS . . ."

In this lesson, we explore our dedication to God within the context of personal and family life. Keep in mind—and frequently point out—that this is a prayer of self-dedication. You may want to ask the group to explore the concept of dedication as a personal commitment to service and worship before discussing the three phrases. You can't go wrong by bringing the conversation back to the notion of our minds, imaginations, and wills as gifts, and by deliberating on how we use these gifts.

ABOUT THE AUTHOR

Nancy Dering Martin has been a teacher, a consultant, an entrepreneur, and a government executive. The thread that runs through these experiences has been her love of leading groups in learning, discovering new directions, and making change for the better. Widely known for her skill in facilitation, she has worked nationally and internationally, engaging people in substantive conversation about issues, ideas, and possibilities and instilling a spirit of inquiry, imagination, and idealism.

It was through her work that Nancy began to think about the potential within the beautiful words of the Episcopal liturgy for helping people grow in wisdom and faith. Jotting down the words, *"Keep watch, dear Lord, with those who work, or watch, or weep this night,"* after Evening Prayer, she began the process of writing this series of books.

Nancy is married to Karl Martin, an education administrator. Together, their family includes five children and seven grandchildren. They enjoy golf and travel and are active in their parish, the Episcopal Cathedral of St. Stephen in Harrisburg, Pennsylvania.